THE STORY BEHIND

# CHOCOLATE

Sean Stewart Price

**Heinemann Library**
**Chicago, Illinois**

Edited by Louise Galpine, Abby Colich, and Laura Knowles
Designed by Philippa Jenkins and Artistix
Original illustrations © Capstone Global Library, LLC 2009
Illustrated by Phil Gleaves and Gary Slater/Specs Art
Picture research by Mica Brancic and Elaine Willis
Originated by Modern Age Repro House Ltd.
Printed in China by CTPS

13 12 11 10
10 9 8 7 6 5 4 3

**Library of Congress Cataloging-in-Publication Data**
Price, Sean Stewart.
  The story behind chocolate / Sean Price. -- 1st ed.
    p. cm. --  (True stories)
  Includes bibliographical references and index.
  ISBN 978-1-4329-2347-1 (hc)
  1. Chocolate--History--Juvenile literature.  I. Title.
  TX767.C5P75 2009
  641.3'374--dc22

                              2008037524

**Acknowledgments**
The author and publishers are grateful to the following
for permission to reproduce copyright material: ©
2008 PhotoLibrary p. **5** (Banana Stock); © Advertising
Archives p. **12**; © Capstone Global Library Ltd p. **iii**
(Tudor Photography); Corbis pp. **10** (© Owen Franken),
**13** (© Bettmann), **15** right (© Wolfgang Kaehler), **15** left
(© Owen Franken), **23** (© Atlantide Phototravel/Massimo
Borchi); Getty Images pp. **4** (© Stockfood Creative/
Jocelyn Demeurs), **6** (© The Bridgeman Art Library/
Mexican School), **17** (© Tyler Hicks), **18–19** (© National
Geographic/James L. Stanfield), **21** (© Iconica/Tim Platt),
**22** (© Iconica/Tom Grill), **25** right (© Iconica/Tom Grill),
**25** left (© National Geographic/James L.); Mary Evans
Picture Library p. **13** (Town & Country Planning); Science
Photo Library p. **24** (© Peter Menzel); The Art Archive
pp. **7** (National Archives Mexico/© Mireille Vautier),
**9** (Musée Jacquemart-André Fontaine-Chaalis/© Gianni
Dagli Orti); The Bridgeman Art Library p. **11** (© Look and
Learn/Private Collection); The Kobal Collection pp. **26–27**
(© Warner Bros./Peter Mountain).

Cover photograph of a chocolate, chocolate powder, cocoa
beans and wooden spoon reproduced with permission of
Photolibrary Group (Photononstop/Fred).

Every effort has been made to contact copyright holders of
any material reproduced in this book. Any omissions will
be rectified in subsequent printings if notice is given to the
publisher.

# Contents

Some words are shown in bold, **like this**.
You can find out what they mean by
looking in the glossary.

# Food of the Gods

▲ The chocolate you eat started out as beans like these.

Rich. Smooth. Sweet. Chocolate is one of those flavors that most people love. Chocolate is often tied to a happy memory. Maybe it is the memory of eating a birthday cake. Or perhaps it is tied to drinking hot **cocoa** on a cold night.

Chocolate's story is a long one. It begins about 3,000 to 4,000 years ago. That is when people discovered the **cacao** (kah-KOW) tree. Back then, it grew in the **rain forests** of Central America and South America. The seeds (also called the beans) of the cacao tree are what become chocolate.

Over time, chocolate's popularity spread. Making and selling chocolate has become a huge business. This is because chocolate is now eaten all over the world. People cannot seem to get enough of it.

## Cacao or cocoa?

The words *cacao* and *cocoa* cause a lot of confusion. In most cases, they mean the same thing. *Cacao* comes from the ancient Native American word for the tree that gives us chocolate products. *Cocoa* started off as a misspelling of *cacao*. But that misspelling became commonly used. Today, many people call the tree and its seeds cacao. But anything made from those seeds is usually called cocoa or chocolate.

◀ Most people enjoy the taste of chocolate.

## How does a scientist say "chocolate tree"?

Scientists give their own names to plants and animals. They always use Latin or Greek words for these names. That way, all scientists use the same name, no matter what language they speak. The scientific name for the cacao tree is *Theobroma cacao*. In Latin, theobroma means "food of the gods."

# The History of Chocolate

▲ **This painting from 1553 shows a Native American pouring chocolate.**

People drank chocolate in ancient times. It is believed that people first tasted chocolate between 1000 and 2000 **BCE**. It happened in the **rain forests** of what is now Mexico, where **cacao** trees grew. Over time, Native American peoples such as the Mayans and Aztecs found that the seeds of the cacao tree could be made into a tasty drink. The Aztecs called the drink xocolatl (zho-KOH-lah-tl).

## Early chocolate

At first, chocolate was not sweet. Chocolate without sugar has a bitter taste. The Mayans and Aztecs did not have sugar but they found ways to make chocolate taste good. They added things such as ground-up peppers and corn. This made the chocolate spicy. The Mayans and Aztecs also liked chocolate to be foamy. They poured it from a great height. This made lots of little bubbles form on top of the drink.

### Yummy money

The Mayans and Aztecs used cacao beans as a type of money. A rabbit could be bought for 10 cacao beans. A **slave** cost 100 beans. The Aztec king Montezuma was rich in cacao beans. He had 100,000 tons of them.

**2000–1000 BCE**
People first taste chocolate.

**1000 BCE–1500 CE**
The Mayan people and their way of life develop.

**2000 BCE**

**1000 BCE**

## Blood and chocolate

The Aztecs believed their chief god needed human blood to keep the sun rising each morning. To get blood, they cut the hearts out of prisoners each day. This was called a human sacrifice. Sometimes the people who were sacrificed learned that they were about to die. When that happened, the Aztecs gave them a special drink. It was chocolate mixed with bloody water. The Aztecs believed this would make the person forget what would happen.

▼ This painting from the 1500s show Aztecs making human sacrifices to the god Mictlantecutli.

| 600 | 1300s–early 1500s | 1502–20 |
|---|---|---|
| The Mayan people set up the first known cacao farms. | The Aztecs rule over Mexico. Their leaders drink chocolate. The Aztecs use cacao beans as money. | Montezuma leads the Aztecs. |

0          1000 CE          2000

## Conquering Mexico

In the late 1400s, European countries began to explore parts of the world that were unknown to them. Led by explorer Hernán Cortés, the Spanish came to Mexico in 1519. The Spanish **conquered** the Aztecs and took over Mexico by 1521. They took cacao beans back to Spain with them in 1528.

## Coming to Europe

Not everyone in Spain liked drinking chocolate. Many people thought that it tasted too bitter, but others enjoyed the flavor.

In the 1600s, chocolate spread around Europe and soon became a favorite drink. The beans still had to be grown in Mexico. That made chocolate very expensive. Only the rich could afford to have it sent across the sea.

## A luxurious treat

Between the 1500s and 1800s, people in Europe found new ways to make chocolate less bitter. They put in cinnamon. Some began to sweeten it with sugar.

During that same period, chocolate became a fun drink for the rich. Wealthy drinkers made special bowls and cups for their chocolate. These dishes were often made of the finest china or silver.

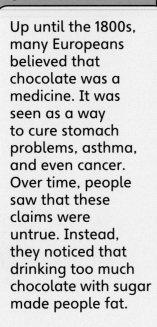

**Chocolate for your health** ✔

Up until the 1800s, many Europeans believed that chocolate was a medicine. It was seen as a way to cure stomach problems, asthma, and even cancer. Over time, people saw that these claims were untrue. Instead, they noticed that drinking too much chocolate with sugar made people fat.

**1519**
Spanish explorer Hernán Cortés arrives in Mexico.

**1521**
The Spanish conquer the Aztecs in Mexico and are introduced to chocolate.

**1528**
The first shipments of cacao beans from Mexico arrive in Spain.

## Chocolate houses

**Chocolate houses** were like restaurants. People could go to drink chocolate and talk to friends. In 1657 the first chocolate house opened in London, England. At first chocolate houses were gathering spots for the rich. But over time, all types of people visited chocolate houses.

▼ Wealthy people could afford to drink chocolate from Mexico.

**1600s**
Chocolate's popularity spreads throughout Europe.

**1657**
The first chocolate house opens in London, England. Chocolate houses spread to other cities and countries.

9

1600

1650

## Improving cocoa

**Cocoa** had some drawbacks as a drink. The cacao beans were full of an oil called **cocoa butter**. The cocoa butter floated to the top of a cup of chocolate. This made the drink greasy. Also, the seeds had to be ground up just right. Otherwise, little chunks of seed floated in the chocolate.

In 1828 the Dutch inventor Coenraad Van Houten found a way to squeeze out the cocoa butter. His invention was called the cocoa press. It is still widely used today.

Chocolate without the cocoa butter is called **cocoa mass**. Cocoa mass could be ground up into cocoa powder. This cocoa powder was much finer and less chunky. It mixed well with hot water and tasted better. That is the type of cocoa we drink today.

◀ Cocoa butter is separated from the cacao beans.

**1750–1850**
The **Industrial Revolution** brings about quicker ways to make and distribute chocolate.

**1795**
Cacao beans are ground up using steam-powered engines for the first time.

# Chocolate becomes a food

Chocolate makers also found a use for the leftover cocoa butter. It could be used to make candy. They mixed cocoa butter with small amounts of cocoa mass and sugar. In 1847 English chocolate maker J. S. Fry created the first chocolate bars. Chocolate bars were cheaper to make than other cocoa products. Chocolate suddenly became affordable for everyone.

## Chocolate and the Industrial Revolution ✔

The early 1800s were a time of great change. People started using machines more than ever before. The new steam engine powered these machines. Machines could grind cocoa better than people could by hand. The machines could also grind more of it faster. This made it possible to make and sell more chocolate products. Newly invented trains helped, too. They moved the chocolate faster to more people.

◄ Trains could carry products quickly between towns.

**1828**
Dutch inventor Coenraad Van Houten creates the cocoa press.

**1847**
English chocolate maker J. S. Fry makes the first chocolate bar.

**Chocolate chips**

In 1930 a Massachusetts dietician (food expert) named Ruth Wakefield put chocolate chunks in her cookie dough. She had invented chocolate chip cookies!

## The business of chocolate

Once people knew how to make chocolate, a series of inventors and businesspeople created a huge international business out of chocolate.

In 1875 the Swiss inventor Daniel Peter mixed powdered milk into cocoa powder. He had created milk chocolate. This became the most popular type of chocolate in candy bars. The German businessman Henri Nestlé had invented powdered milk earlier, in the 1860s. Nestlé used his invention to form his own company. His company, Nestlé, went on to become one of the world's biggest makers of milk chocolate.

In 1879 Swiss inventor Rodolphe Lindt invented a grinding process called conching. It made chocolate smoother and easier to eat. Conching is still used today.

▶ In this poster from the 1900s, a picture of a milkmaid is used to advertise Cadbury's milk chocolate.

**1824**
John Cadbury opens a small chocolate shop in London, England.

**1860s**
German businessman Henri Nestlé invents powdered milk.

**1875**
Swiss inventor Daniel Peter invents milk chocolate.

**1879**
Swiss inventor Rodolphe Lindt invents a grinding process called conching.

1850

**BIOGRAPHY**

**The British Hershey**

In 1824 John Cadbury opened a small shop in London, England, that sold chocolate drinks. Over time, the Cadbury family became the largest chocolate maker in the United Kingdom.

## Milton S. Hershey

Milton S. Hershey helped bring chocolate to the United States. In the 1890s he made his first chocolate bars. Hershey went on to create new ways to **mass-produce** candy bars. He soon owned the largest chocolate company in the United States. Over time, his company, Hershey's, created well-known products such as Hershey Bars and Hershey's Kisses.

## Competition

U.S. candy maker Frank C. Mars founded the Mars Company in 1911. It became the main rival of Hershey's in the United States.

The companies begun by Mars and these other inventors and businesspeople continue to be big business today.

**1890s**

Pennsylvania candy maker Milton Hershey makes his first chocolate bars. Hershey's company becomes one of the world's largest chocolate companies.

1900

**1930**

U.S. dietician Ruth Wakefield invents chocolate chip cookies.

13

1950

# From Cacao Tree to Candy Bar

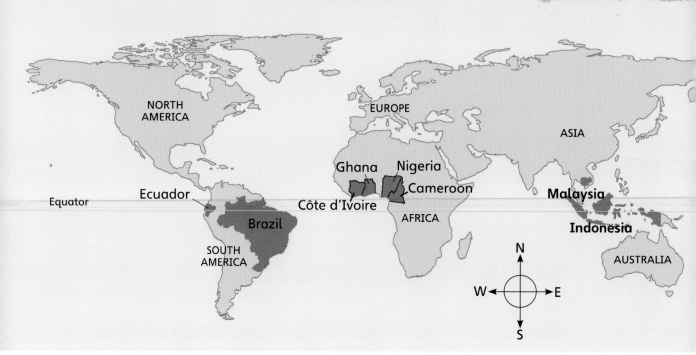

NORTH AMERICA

EUROPE

ASIA

Ghana Nigeria

Cameroon

Ecuador

Côte d'Ivoire

Malaysia

Equator

Brazil

AFRICA

Indonesia

SOUTH AMERICA

AUSTRALIA

N

W ← → E

S

▲ The brown areas on this world map show the main cacao growing countries. 75 percent of all cacao beans are grown in countries in Africa.

All chocolate starts off on **cacao** trees. These trees grow in **tropical rain forests**. Such rain forests are mostly found near the equator. This is the imaginary line that runs east and west along Earth's center (see map).

Cacao trees need the rain forests' heat and moisture. They also need shade. Tall trees grow over cacao trees. These "mother trees" protect cacao trees from too much sunlight and moisture.

## World travelers

The first cacao trees probably grew in South America's rain forests. Since then, humans have spread them. Most cacao trees today grow in Africa. Many rain forests are becoming endangered. People burn them on purpose. They do this so they can plant crops such as corn. Others cut down trees for lumber (wood).

Destroying rain forests kills off many important plants and animals. It also leaves fewer places to grow cacao trees.

## Pods

Cacao **pods** grow directly off the trunk and main branches of the tree. Pods start off green. After about four months, they turn red, yellow, or orange. That means they are ready to be picked. Each pod contains about 40 seeds (beans).

> **Another sweet surprise**
>
> In their pods, cacao beans are surrounded by a sticky white fluid. This white fluid is sweet. People like to drink it, but it tastes nothing like chocolate.

▲ Cacao trees grow pink and white flowers.

◀ These are the pods in which cacao beans grow. The pod on the left has been cut in half. The white parts inside are the beans.

15

## Cacao farms and plantations

Cacao trees are often grown on **plantations**, or large farms. Workers collect the pods off the trees.

Working with cacao trees can be dangerous. Workers use big knives called machetes. These are used to cut down cacao pods. Workers also get sprayed with pesticides. These are chemicals used to kill bugs. Pesticides can harm people's eyes, skin, and **nerves**.

## The dark side of chocolate

Chocolate farms and plantations have long been tied to slavery. Starting in the 1600s, **slaves** were used on cacao plantations. Over time, most types of slavery ended. But in 1999, reporters found that some types still exist. Children in Africa are often bought and sold. Many become workers on cacao farms. Some children are sold to African cacao farms by their parents. Other parents make their children work for them. In both cases, the parents are very poor. They need the money to survive.

### Child labor

The problem of child labor is hard to solve. Companies cannot just stop buying cacao beans. Many children need to work at least some of the time. If they do not, their families will starve. The problem of child labor cannot end overnight. Countries in Africa must make child labor illegal. They must also build schools for child workers. These changes will give children a better life.

▶ Many poor children have to work on cacao plantations to help feed their family. They must cut down pods and collect the beans.

## Preparing the beans

After workers at the farm or plantation have taken the pods off the trees, they split the pods open and take out the beans. They put the beans in a dark place to **ferment**. As they ferment, the beans undergo chemical changes that make them taste better. Without this, there would be no chocolate flavor. Then the beans dry in the sun. After about two weeks, the beans are shipped to chocolate-making factories.

## At the factory

Chocolate makers have the beans roasted, or cooked over steady heat. This helps bring out the chocolate flavor.

▼ Chocolate must be stirred up well before it is ready to be made into chocolate bars.

Then, the beans are winnowed. This means the beans' hard outer shells are removed. Only the insides, or "nibs," are left. The nibs are ground up. This turns them into an oily paste. Heat is added to melt it into a liquid called **cocoa mass**. To make **cocoa**, the cocoa mass is pressed to remove the **cocoa butter**. To make a chocolate bar, cocoa mass is mixed with more cocoa butter, along with sugar and milk.

For chocolate bars, the chocolate then goes through a second grinding and is mixed well. It is heated and mixed well again to give it a glossy look when it dries. The chocolate is poured into molds to make chocolate bars. The bars are wrapped, shipped, and sold.

**Hungry for chocolate**

Chocolate candy is one of the most popular foods in the world. As just one example, more than 400 million M&Ms are made each day.

# What's in Chocolate?

KEY

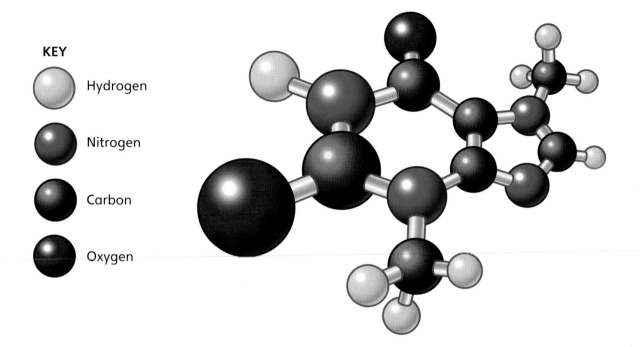

Hydrogen

Nitrogen

Carbon

Oxygen

▲ The chemical theobromine is the active ingredient in chocolate. It is made up of oxygen, nitrogen, carbon, and hydrogen **atoms**.

## The chemistry of chocolate

People love chocolate. Eating chocolate seems to lift people's spirits.

The reason for this lift is a chemical called theobromine (see diagram). Theobromine is the active ingredient in chocolate. The active ingredient is the most important chemical within something.

Theobromine is a mild **stimulant.** But it is not the only stimulant. Chocolate also contains caffeine. Caffeine is the same stimulant found in coffee and soft drinks. However, chocolate has much less caffeine than coffee or soft drinks.

Some chemicals in chocolate are healthy. Scientists believe that chemicals called antioxidants in dark chocolate can lower a person's blood pressure. That is an important health benefit. High blood pressure can cause strokes and other serious illnesses.

## Chocolate's drawbacks

Many chocolate products can also harm a person's health. Most chocolate products contain a lot of **fat**. Also, most of them have sugar added. Fat and sugar cause people to gain weight. Eating too much chocolate can cause people to be severely overweight.

Chocolate is fine to eat in small amounts, but too much of it will harm your health.

### Chocolate allergies ✔

Many people think that they are **allergic** to chocolate. However, very few people are allergic to chocolate itself. Usually they are allergic to something that has been added to chocolate. That can include milk or nuts.

▼ Theobromine poisons dogs and other animals, including horses. Even a small taste of chocolate can kill them. Keep chocolate away from pets.

# Types of chocolate

Chocolate comes in many different flavors. Here are some of the most popular.

### Milk chocolate

Milk chocolate is the type of chocolate found in most candy bars. It is mostly **cocoa** and **cocoa butter**, mixed with milk and sugar.

### White chocolate

White chocolate is made up mostly of cocoa butter. It has little or no **cocoa mass**. In fact, many chocolate makers do not even consider this to be chocolate. White chocolate also contains sugar, milk, and vanilla.

### Dark chocolate

▼ These chocolates contain different amounts of cocoa mass.

Dark chocolate is sweetened chocolate with a lot of cocoa mass. This creates a dark color. Dark chocolate usually contains little milk.

## Sweet dark chocolate and semi-sweet chocolate

Sweet dark chocolate and semi-sweet chocolate are dark chocolates that are usually used for baking. They are often used to make cakes and brownies.

▲ Fine chocolates come in many beautiful designs.

## Bittersweet chocolate

Bittersweet chocolate is a type of very dark chocolate. It is mostly cocoa mass, with just a little sugar. It is also used for baking things such as cakes and pastries.

## Unsweetened chocolate

Unsweetened chocolate is chocolate in its rawest form. It tastes very bitter because it has no sugar. It is sprinkled over salads and also used to thicken sauces.

### Fine chocolates

Fine chocolates cost a lot of money. They are usually made from dark chocolate, which tastes very rich. Fine chocolates are made from carefully selected **cacao** beans. Then the beans are prepared to bring out maximum flavor.

Some of the world's most expensive chocolates come from the Knipschildt Chocolatier in Norwalk, Connecticut. One mouthful can cost several hundred dollars. One pound can cost several thousand dollars.

# The World of Chocolate

Chocolate's popularity spans the globe. Some dishes are sweet, but others are not sweet at all. Here are just a few favorites from around the world.

## Black Forest cake

Black Forest cake (or gateau) is one of Germany's most famous desserts. It is made up of layers of chocolate cake. Between each layer are whipped cream and cherries.

► In some countries, scorpions, crickets, ants, grasshoppers, and other bugs are on the menu. Many insects are healthy to eat. They taste good covered in chocolate.

## Mole

Mole is a Mexican sauce that is made using unsweetened chocolate. Mole can include ingredients like cinnamon, onions, and tomatoes. A mole can be spread over chicken or pork.

## Green tea chocolate balls

On Valentine's Day in Japan, girls give boys chocolate treats. They often include green tea chocolate balls. The white chocolate inside offsets the bitter taste of the ground-up tea.

### Chocolate and holidays

Chocolate is a big part of many holidays. At Easter, Christian children in many countries eat chocolate bunnies or eggs. At Hanukkah, Jewish children receive presents of chocolate coins wrapped in gold foil. On the Day of the Dead, a Mexican holiday to remember those who have died, children munch on chocolate skulls. On Halloween, U.S. children get bags full of candy by "trick-or-treating."

▲ Chocolate coins are given to Jewish children at Hanukkah.

◀ Chocolate cooks like to outdo one another. Many make chocolate sculptures. This cook has made a giant chocolate model of the Statue of Liberty.

# Inspired by Chocolate

Chocolate naturally makes people think of eating. But it has filled our lives with many other kinds of good things.

## Movies and books

Chocolate often has a starring role in movies and books. One of the most famous is the book *Charlie and the Chocolate Factory* by British author Roald Dahl. It has twice been made into a movie. The story centers around a poor boy named Charlie Bucket. He wins a trip to tour a magical chocolate factory. It is owned by the talented chocolate maker Willy Wonka.

## A big discovery

Chocolate played a key role in a well-known invention. Around 1946, U.S. inventor Percy L. Spencer was touring a factory. He stopped in front of a device. It sent out invisible energy waves called microwaves. Spencer was carrying a chocolate bar in one of his pockets. Suddenly, he felt the candy melt as if it had been put in a hot oven. That gave Spencer an idea. He went on to invent the microwave oven.

▲ In Willy Wonka's chocolate factory, even grass and trees are made out of chocolate and candy.

## Health care products

**Cocoa butter** is the **fat** that gets squeezed out of chocolate. It keeps its shape at room temperature. But it melts at body temperature. That makes it perfect for putting in skin care products. Cocoa butter can be found in lotions, sunscreens, makeup, soaps, and shampoos. It is also used to prevent chapped lips and to give moisture to dry skin.

So, chocolate touches more than just our stomachs. Yet it is first and foremost something that tastes great. Chocolate gives us cool treats and warm memories. There is no other food quite like it.

# Timeline

(These dates are often approximations.)

**2000–1000 BCE**
People first taste chocolate.

2000 BCE · · · · · · 1500 BCE

**1502–20**
Montezuma leads the Aztecs.

**1300s–early 1500s**
The Aztecs rule over Mexico. Their leaders drink chocolate. The Aztecs use cacao beans as money.

1500

**1519**
Spanish explorer Hernán Cortés arrives in Mexico.

**1521**
The Spanish **conquer** the Aztecs in Mexico and are introduced to chocolate.

**1528**
The first shipments of cacao beans from Mexico arrive in Spain.

1550

**1657**
The first **chocolate house** opens in London, England. Chocolate houses spread to other cities and countries.

1700

**1750–1850**
The **Industrial Revolution** brings about quicker ways to make and distribute chocolate.

**1753**
The cacao tree is given the scientific name *Theobroma cacao*.

1750

**1890s**
Pennsylvania candy maker Milton Hershey makes his first chocolate bars.

**1879**
Swiss inventor Rodolphe Lindt invents a grinding process called conching.

**1875**
Swiss inventor Daniel Peter invents milk chocolate.

1900

**1930**
U.S. dietician (food expert) Ruth Wakefield invents chocolate chip cookies.

1950

28    This symbol shows where there is a change of scale in the timeline, or where a long period of time with no noted events has been left out.

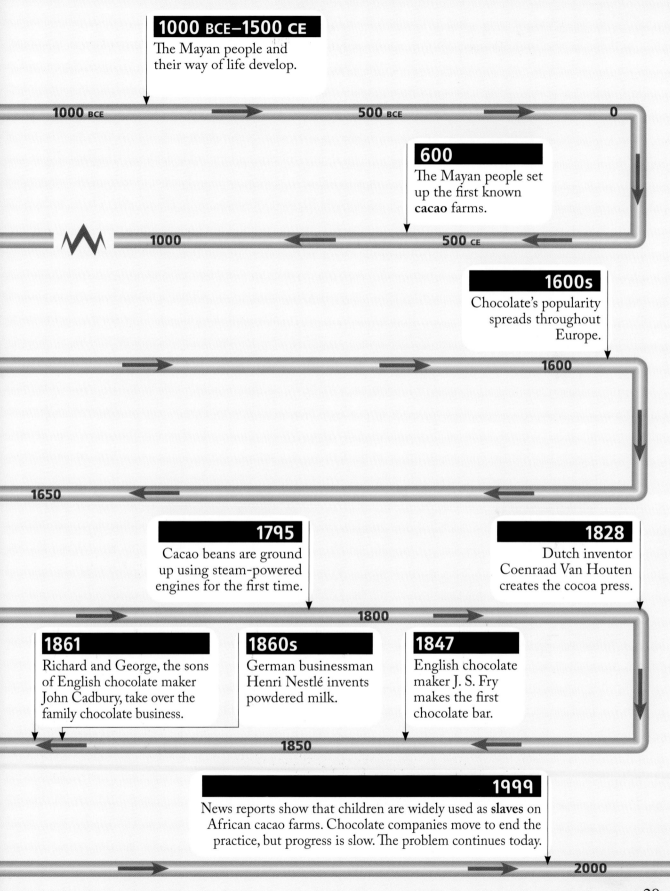

**1000 BCE–1500 CE**
The Mayan people and their way of life develop.

1000 BCE

500 BCE

0

**600**
The Mayan people set up the first known **cacao** farms.

1000

500 CE

**1600s**
Chocolate's popularity spreads throughout Europe.

1600

1650

**1795**
Cacao beans are ground up using steam-powered engines for the first time.

**1828**
Dutch inventor Coenraad Van Houten creates the cocoa press.

1800

**1861**
Richard and George, the sons of English chocolate maker John Cadbury, take over the family chocolate business.

**1860s**
German businessman Henri Nestlé invents powdered milk.

**1847**
English chocolate maker J. S. Fry makes the first chocolate bar.

1850

**1999**
News reports show that children are widely used as **slaves** on African cacao farms. Chocolate companies move to end the practice, but progress is slow. The problem continues today.

2000

# Glossary

**allergic** when people get sick after eating or being near to something. Allergy problems can include headaches and rashes.

**atom** one of the smallest units that make up substances. Chocolate is made up of millions of atoms.

**BCE** meaning "before the common era." When this appears after a date, it refers to the time before the Christian religion began. BCE dates are always counted backwards.

**cacao** word that is often used to refer to chocolate products. The word *cocoa* comes from *cacao* and means the same thing.

**CE** meaning "common era." When this appears after a date, it refers to the time after the Christian religion began.

**chocolate house** type of meeting place popular from the 1600s to the 1800s. People went to chocolate houses to eat and drink chocolate products.

**cocoa** word that is often used to refer to chocolate products. The word *cocoa* comes from *cacao* and means the same thing.

**cocoa butter** fat found in cacao beans. Cocoa butter is used to make many chocolate products such as candy bars.

**cocoa mass** cacao beans that have been ground up or melted. Cocoa mass is used to make chocolate products.

**conquer** take over by force. The Spanish conquered the Aztecs in Mexico.

**fat** greasy oil found in animals and plants. Cocoa butter is the fat from cacao beans.

**ferment** age and almost rot in order to create chemical changes

**Industrial Revolution** period from about 1750 to 1850. The Industrial Revolution was a period of great change because of new inventions such as the steam engine and telegraph.

**mass-produce** make a large number of items quickly and at low cost. Candy bars are mass-produced by chocolate companies.

**nerve** part of the body that senses things such as heat and motion. Nerves help carry information to the brain.

**plantation** large farm. Cacao beans are often grown on plantations.

**pod** pouch produced by a plant that contains seeds. Cacao trees grow seeds within pods.

**rain forest** forest near the equator where there is a lot of heat and rain. Cacao trees grow in rain forests.

**slave** person who is forced to work for no pay. In some parts of Africa, slaves are still used to pick cacao pods.

**stimulant** chemical that makes people more alert and aware for a short time. Chocolate contains mild stimulants.

**tropical** region of the Earth near the equator. Tropical regions are very hot and humid.

# Find Out More

## Books

Bennett, Leonie. *The Life of George Cadbury*. Chicago: Heinemann Library, 2005.

Gillis, Jennifer Blizin. *Milton Hershey: The Founder of Hershey's Chocolate*. Chicago: Heinemann Library, 2005.

Morganelli, Adrianna. *The Biography of Chocolate*. New York: Crabtree, 2005.

Polin, C. J. *The Story of Chocolate*. New York: DK, 2005.

## Websites

Explore this great history of chocolate from the Field Museum in Chicago.
**www.fieldmuseum.org/Chocolate/history.html**

Check out this history from the Exploratorium in San Francisco.
**www.exploratorium.edu/chocolate**

Take a virtual tour of a chocolate factory.
**www.grenadachocolate.com/tour/process1.html**

## Places to Visit

Hershey Museum
170 West Hersheypark Drive
Hershey, PA 17033
www.hersheystory.org

Visit the Hershey Museum to find out the history behind Milton Hershey and his chocolate factory.

# Index